BIOGRAPHIES

Lydia Larson I BEN
Theatre includes: *Skin A Cat* (VAULT Festival); *We Have Fallen* (InSite); *The After-Dinner Joke*, *Springs Eternal* (Orange Tree); *Persuasion* (Salisbury Playhouse); *24 Hour Plays* (Old Vic); *Pride and Prejudice* (Theatre Royal Bath); *Arcadia* (SF Productions).

Television includes: *Doctors* (BBC); *Kidnapped* (Virgin); *Routes* (Channel 4).

Pierro Niel-Mee I ANNA
Theatre includes: *The Spring Tide* (Old Red Lion); *Wolf Hall* and *Bring Up the Bodies* (Royal Shakespeare Company, Aldwych/Winter Garden); *Kenny Morgan* (Arcola).

Television includes: *The Bastard Executioner* (FX); *Casualty* (BBC); *Inspector Lewis*, *Bouquet of Barbed Wire* (ITV); *Little Crackers* (Sky 1).

Film includes: *Death of a Farmer*, *City of Life*.

Emily Burns I Director
As Director: *Scenes from the End* (Tristan Bates); *Much Ado About Nothing* (Cambridge American Stage tour); *Esio Trot* (Assembly Studios).

As Assistant Director: *The Snow Maiden*, *Rheingold*, *Siegfried* (Opera North); *Platonov*, *Ivanov*, *The Seagull* (Chichester Festival Theatre); *Don't Dress for Dinner* (Thousand Islands Playhouse); *Upper Cut* (Southwark Playhouse).

Liam Williams I Writer
Liam Williams is a writer, comedian and actor known primarily for his stand-up shows and work with sketch group Sheeps. His self-titled debut show was nominated for the Edinburgh Comedy Best Newcomer Award in 2013, and a year later his follow-up show *Capitalism* earned a nomination for the main award and critical acclaim including a five-star review from the *Guardian* who described the show as 'an extraordinary cri-de-couer'. That same year the *Independent* suggested Williams might be 'the comic voice of a generation'.

His writing credits include: *Comedy Blaps* (Channel 4); *From Fact to Fiction: Purple Saturday*, *Ladhood*, *The Now Show* (Radio 4); *People Time* (BBC Three); *Charlie Brooker's 2015 Wipe* (BBC Two); *2016: Year Friends* (Vimeo – Staff Pick).

Travesty is Liam's debut play.

F I G H T IN THE D O G

Small company. Big shows.

Fight in the Dog was established with the intention of bridging the gap between the worlds of theatre and comedy. The company's chief aim is to create work that's at once as funny as the best comedy and as thought-provoking as the best theatre – innovative, provocative, experimental and surprising.

Fight in the Dog was formed after a supposedly small and relaxed charity production of *Twelfth Night* got out of hand and sold out a 600-seater theatre and raised almost £9k for the charity Refugee Action. That production of *Twelfth Night* has since transferred to Latitude Festival and London Wonderground on the Southbank.

The team behind Fight in the Dog are Matt Bulmer, Isobel David, Bríd Kirby and Liam Williams.

'It's not the size of the dog in the fight, it's the size of the fight in the dog.' *Mark Twain*

www.fightinthedog.co.uk

Fight in the Dog would like to thank:

Daran Johnson, Matt Bulmer, The Invisible Dot, Simon Pearce, Hannah Martin, Charlie Perkins, Ali Hunter, Alexander Owen, Laura Jayne Ayres, Luke Sumner, Sarah Twomey, Jade Williams, Joshua James, Mark Milligan, Tania Harrison, Latitude Festival, Alby Bailey, Nina Cosford, David, Sophie and Helen at the New Diorama Theatre, Zoe Robinson, The Hippodrome Casino, Fergus Crook, The Landor Pub, Tallulah Brown, Theatre503, Beth Rad, Veronique Baxter, Al Roberts, Kitty Laing, Ciaran Clarke.

Thanks to all our supporters to date: Flora Anderson, Craig Angus, Blink Industries, Rosana Bosana, Alex Bower, Alex Bowler, Colin Bowles, Don Boyd, Adam Bracy, Michael Bramley, Patrick Brooks, Ian Burns, David Byrne, Caroline Chartier, Ken Cheng, Alex Cotham, Gus Crook, Serafina Cusack, Lizzie Donnelly, Ciaran Dowd, Gilbert Dowding, Eliot Fallows, Will Farrell, Lucy Fitzgerald, Katy Funnell, Claire Haigh, Jacob Hawley, Busby Humblebee, David Isaacs, Miki Inamura, Mark Jones, Olga Kokh, Liam Lonergan, Ian MacArthur, Penny Matthews, Charles Miller, Ste Montgomery, Sarah Musselbrook, Clare O'Connor, Benjamin Partridge, E Paston, Joseph Pelling , Hannah Pescod, Hannah Platt, Katie Pope, Rebecca Ptazynski, Oliver Refson, Charlotte Ritchie, Katie Rogers, Tom Rosenthal, Robin Seamer, Barry Shapiro, Callum Smith, Moses Ssebandeke, Mike Stuart, George Sully, Freddie Syborn, Azam Taiyeb, Richard Tyson, Heloise Werner, Dougal Wilson, Lizzie White, Lucien Young.

TRAVESTY

Liam Williams

Characters

ANNA, *mid-late twenties, to be played by a man*
BEN, *mid-late twenties, to be played by a woman*

A Note on Scene Changes

The action during scene changes should contribute to the telling of the story. The audience should feel not as if they are just watching actors move props around, but as if they are watching the characters interact and get on with their lives during the phases between scenes, almost montage-style.

This text went to press before the end of rehearsals and so may differ slightly from the play as performed.

One

A bedroom. Day. BEN *is in bed, looking at* ANNA *who is standing with her back to him, topless, pulling on pyjama trousers. She turns around, and covers her breasts as she looks on the floor for something.* BEN *places a used tissue on the table next to the bed.*

BEN. Can I smoke in here?

ANNA. No! I've just moved in. I don't know why you feel the need to smoke after sex. It's not 1991.

He laughs dryly. Puts cig back in packet.

Can I wear your jumper?

BEN. Don't get too attached. Gotta go in a minute.

She picks his jumper off the floor and puts it on. She hops into bed. They snuggle up happily, if a little awkwardly.

Pause.

ANNA. Should we have used a condom?

BEN. I feel like that's becoming a bit of a catchphrase.

ANNA. It's so bad. I just get too consumed.

BEN. Ha, 'consumed'. You're a little poet. Do I consume you with my manly jaws. (*Climbs on top of her.*) And... heft?

ANNA. It's nice for it to feel consuming. Doesn't happen with everyone.

He laughs quietly and seems suddenly contemplative.

You alright?

BEN. Yeah fine, why?

ANNA. What's up?

BEN. When you say it 'doesn't happen with everyone'…

ANNA. Huh?

BEN. You get consumed by sex with me and it doesn't happen with everyone.

ANNA. Yeah.

BEN. Who's 'everyone' then?

ANNA. Just… other people.

BEN. So this 'everyone' is still on the scene, are they?

ANNA. I thought you didn't care.

BEN. Why do you say that?

ANNA. Last night in the restaurant I started talking about a guy I went on a date with a while back?

He doesn't seem to remember.

I said: 'Sorry, is it weird to talk about him?' and you said 'Nah I don't care…'

BEN *pretends not to remember for a second and then…*

BEN (*faux-offhand*). Oh the… video fella.

ANNA. Documentary-maker. Seb.

BEN. No I don't care. Just trying to make pillow talk. So… erm – (*Ironising a pillow-talk cliché.*) what's your favourite song?

ANNA. Wait, so are *you*?

BEN. Am I what?

ANNA. Are you sleeping with other girls?

BEN. Erm…

ANNA. Ben.

BEN. I, yeah, sometimes.

ANNA (*pulling away from him*). We should be using a condom.

BEN. No wait. I'm not… I'm clean.

ANNA. How do you know?

BEN. Because, I know… I only sleep with people who are…

ANNA. Go on.

BEN (*deliberate, bad-taste humour*). Like, middle class.

ANNA. Ah. That's fucking snobbish.

BEN. I'm joking.

ANNA. Sure. I know you pride yourself on your humble working-class origins.

BEN. No I pride myself on my humble lower-middle-class origins. But like really low. Like we had a Škoda.

ANNA. How do you know I haven't got AIDS?

Slight pause.

BEN. I guess I assume.

ANNA. Ridiculous man.

BEN. You must have assumed too. Anyway, you know, you don't need to worry about… babies… cos you know.

With his head he gives a vague gesture intended to signify pulling out early but it doesn't really end up signifying anything.

ANNA. I was thinking of getting the coil.

BEN. Oh right.

ANNA. I'm too young to be a mumma.

BEN. How old are you?

ANNA. Twenty-five. What are you, twenty-nine?

BEN (*bit offended*). I'm twenty-eight!

He nods. They reflect on this information for a few seconds.

ANNA (*bit sarcastic*). High-end pillow talk.

BEN. Well what is your favourite song?

ANNA (*amused*). Erm… maybe… a Leonard Cohen one.

BEN (*sung, loudly*). 'I heard there was a secret chord!'

ANNA. No, not that one.

> *He starts singing 'Hey, That's No Way to Say Goodbye'.*
> *He doesn't really know it, she sings along with him, teaching*
> *him the words.*

Do you serenade all your sexual partners?

BEN. Not this again. Anyway, it's not a serenade. It's an aubade.

ANNA. Aubade? What's that? What's the difference?

BEN. A serenade is a song of seduction. Typically sung at night. An aubade is sung the morning after. A song of farewell.

ANNA. Farewell?

BEN. For now.

> *He gets up. Starts looking for his things.*

Right. I gotta go.

ANNA (*plaintive*). Why?

BEN. I've got loads of marking to do.

ANNA. Why don't you do it later?

BEN. I'm hanging out with Amir later. You'll be alright. Why don't you lie in bed all day and watch *Made in Chelsea*?

ANNA. I do watch other things you know. Maybe I'll watch Seb's new documentary about education in rural China.

BEN. You seen my other trainer?

> *She doesn't look.*

ANNA. Amir is the guy you came to the party with, right?

BEN. Yeah he lived with Caroline when we were at uni. I used to go round there a lot.

ANNA. Oh yeah. She said.

BEN. What do you mean 'she said'? What did she say?

ANNA. Nothing, she just said you went round there a lot.

BEN (*bit suspicious*). How do you know Caroline again?

ANNA. School.

BEN. Right. Yeah. It's weird how public-school people all stay friends for life.

ANNA. Are you not still friends with anybody you went to school with?

BEN. Nope. They're all in Wolverhampton having shit lives.

ANNA. Snobbish.

BEN. No it isn't. Can I have my jumper please?

ANNA. In a minute. Is Amir your best friend?

BEN. I guess so. Why?

ANNA. I could just tell. When he left the party you seemed a bit lost.

BEN (*almost offended*). Lost?

ANNA. Not, lost I dunno, just…

BEN. Bored probably.

ANNA. Are you not very sociable?

BEN. Yeah I am. I've got friends.

ANNA. How many?

BEN (*laughs*). I dunno. Amir…

ANNA. Yeah…

BEN. My friend Gillian.

Pause.

ANNA. So two.

BEN. I'm not gonna list all my friends. How many friends have you got?

ANNA. Seventy-five.

BEN. Precise.

ANNA. That's how many people were in my year at school.

He laughs.

BEN. Give me my jumper now.

ANNA. No!

Playfully he begins trying to wrestle it off her. Giddily she resists.

BEN. Give it to me!

ANNA. No I wanna keep it.

BEN. No it's my favourite jumper. I'll bring you a different one next time.

She considers this for a second.

ANNA. What if I told you you can't see me any more if you're sleeping with other people?

BEN. You wouldn't.

ANNA. What would you do?

BEN. Dunno.

ANNA. It's not an ultimatum. Just interested.

Pause. BEN *thinks. Bemused. Almost amused.*

BEN. I dunno why you're so bothered.

ANNA. I like hanging out with you. I like, y'know, doing everything with you.

She kisses him, sincerely.

I like hanging out with you. I like your smell.

BEN. What smell?

ANNA. I dunno, it's like…

She sniffs his temple gently. [*Here the actors should improvise identifying one another's bodily aromas.*]

BEN. Sorry what were you saying – you like hanging out with me?

ANNA. Yes. I like doing everything with you. And I don't just want you to leave immediately afterwards. It's just fun! Isn't it?

BEN. Yeah… but… you can have fun with one person one day, and then…

ANNA. No.

BEN. What?

ANNA. It won't be fun any more if I know you're seeing other people.

BEN. So it is an ultimatum.

ANNA. I need a shower. Here's your precious jumper.

She gets up and takes the jumper off. Pause.

BEN. Maybe I could do with a shower actually. I'll come with you.

ANNA. No way.

BEN. Why not?

ANNA. I don't know you well enough to let you shower with me.

BEN. You've slept with me three times. I fingered you in a bathroom.

ANNA. Ben!

BEN. We've been to the fair!

ANNA. You can't shower with me. It's too intimate.

BEN. Showering together is more intimate than sleeping together?

ANNA. Yes!

BEN. How is it?

ANNA. Have you ever slept with somebody but then not showered with them?

BEN. Course.

ANNA. But have you ever showered with someone but not slept with them.

BEN. Not including family?

ANNA. Obviously.

BEN *ponders this. Seriously.*

BEN. No.

ANNA. There you go then. It's a rarer privilege. I'm hungry.

BEN. Why do feel like you don't know me?

ANNA. Because I don't. Not really. And you don't really know me.

BEN. I do… I know you're twenty-five, you work in PR. I know you went to Leeds and did… Hissss –

ANNA. / Psychology.

BEN. Psychology.

ANNA. You studied English, didn't you?

BEN. Yup.

ANNA. What's your favourite book?

BEN. That's an impossible question.

ANNA. Wow. All right. Well what book would you choose on *Desert Island Discs*?

He thinks for a couple of seconds.

BEN. *The Norton Anthology of English Literature*.

ANNA. Boring.

BEN. What would yours be?

ANNA. Hmm. Probably *To Kill a Mockingbird*.

BEN. A solid text.

ANNA. What else do you know about me?

BEN. You're from the South.

ANNA. Wow, I can't believe you remembered I'm from the South.

BEN. Oxford. A village called... Abingdon.

    ANNA *looks faintly impressed for a second.*

ANNA. Good memory. (*Changing tone.*) But that's just like my CV. I meant you don't know who I really am.

BEN. I know you don't want to work in PR; you want to be a psychologist.

ANNA. Psychotherapist.

BEN. A psychotherapist.

ANNA. Or a psychologist. I don't know really.

BEN. I know you like risotto.

ANNA. Yeah I should probably curb that habit.

BEN. Why?

ANNA. I'm getting a belly.

BEN. No you're not. Even if you were so what?

ANNA. Hmm. What else do you claim to know about me?

BEN. I know you live with Caroline. How do you have such a nice flat by the way?

ANNA. My parents own it.

BEN. Oh. (*Stifling his amusement, taking in the property.*) You're set up for life then.

ANNA. No. Only for three years.

BEN. Why?

ANNA. My brother will move in when he graduates.

BEN. Poor you. What do your parents do?

ANNA. Dad works for BP.

BEN. In a petrol station?

ANNA. No. (*Beat.*) He's a director.

BEN. How about your mum?

ANNA. I dunno. She raised me and my brother…

BEN (*ironic tone*). Well raising kids is a full-time job!

ANNA (*sincere*). It is in a way.

BEN. Yeah I know. Just kidding.

ANNA. What do yours do?

BEN. They both work for the NHS.

ANNA. Are they doctors?

BEN. Nope. Admin.

ANNA. Oh. Are they still together?

BEN. Oh yeah. They love it.

ANNA. Love what?

BEN. Marriage. Can't get enough of it. How about yours?

ANNA. Yeah they're still together. I sometimes wonder if they just can't be arsed getting divorced.

BEN. That's sad.

ANNA. I think it's quite normal isn't it?

BEN. What, staying in an unhappy marriage?

ANNA. Not unhappy. Just not… happy.

BEN. Probably. I think it's getting less common though. With the divorce rate going up.

ANNA. The divorce rate's actually going down.

BEN. Is it?

ANNA. Yeah I read it the other day.

BEN (*almost disbelieving*). Well I don't know about that.

ANNA. Well I do, I read about it the other day.

He makes a disbelieving face.

BEN. Well anyway. Just as a society we're maybe realising that transcendental, monogamous lifelong love isn't really a viable solution to the existential problems inherent to the human condition.

ANNA. So you talk like that even when you're sober?

Pause. He lingers by the door.

BEN. Where's Caroline today?

ANNA. She'll be at Tom's. Her boyfriend's. Caroline finds it weird I've been seeing you, by the way.

BEN. Why?

ANNA. She didn't go into it. I just told her we went to the fair and she said 'oh that's weird'.

BEN. Weird that we went to the fair?

ANNA. No, weird that we went anywhere. Just weird that we went out.

BEN *takes this in.*

BEN. What's Caroline's problem though? She doesn't even know me. She just happened to live with Amir at uni and she just happens to live with you and you just happened to have a housewarming party that I just happened to be and we just happened to get on. Then I fingered you in a toilet. Then we went to the fair and then had sex and then we went for dinner and then had sex. (*Beat.*) And now here we are.

ANNA. Yep. And now you're leaving. Apparently.

BEN. I wanna know why Caroline thinks this is weird.

ANNA. I guess she just meant weird like surprising, because, as you say, she doesn't really know you and you happened to be at her party but you're not really part of our usual group of friends, so.

BEN. Well I don't wanna be.

ANNA. Didn't say you did.

BEN. Poshos.

ANNA (*posh voice*). I'm not posh!

BEN (*mocking posh voice*). I'm not posh!

ANNA. Fuck off! I dunno why'd you sleep with me if you hate posh people so much.

BEN. You're just too bewitching. Anyway, I've got posh friends. I'm just saying a lot of those lot are like pretentiously posh.

ANNA. Why?

BEN. They're like... documentary-makers... and...

ANNA. Maybe they think you're pretentious?

BEN. I'm pretentious?!

ANNA. Or a bit grandiose maybe.

BEN. Grandiose?! I'm an English teacher for fuck's sake!

ANNA. I know...

BEN. At a state school.

ANNA. Yes but you've got a way...

BEN. A way...

ANNA. Like a way of... speaking... of being... I dunno you're like – (*Does impression*.) 'Ooh I'm from the Midlands and I like poetry and I'm very political.'

BEN. It's hard not to be at the moment.

ANNA. I manage it somehow.

BEN. I imagine you're quite centrist.

    ANNA *shrugs*.

    Or are you just apathetic?

ANNA. No. I do care about stuff.

BEN. What do you care about?

    She thinks.

ANNA. People.

BEN. What people?

ANNA. Friends. Family.

BEN. So just people you know?

ANNA. It's harder to care about people I don't know, isn't it?

BEN. So you don't care about all the people suffering unjustly in the world? In this country for fuck's sake!

ANNA. Of course I do. There's just not much I can do to help them. So I try to save my energy trying to help people I do know. If they need help.

BEN. Fair enough. So what else has Caroline said about me?

ANNA. Nothing.

BEN. Nothing at all?

ANNA. Oh, she said you like lemon tart.

BEN. Did she?!

ANNA. Yeah she said it's the only food you eat.

BEN. It's not the only food I eat!

ANNA. Well maybe it's the only food she ever saw you eat.

    BEN *ponders this*.

BEN. She must have seen me have some crisps or something at some point.

ANNA. She didn't mention it.

BEN. So she didn't tell you anything else?

ANNA (*exasperated*). I dunno. She said you're an English teacher.

BEN. Well I told you that.

ANNA. Yeah and you told me you don't want to be an English teacher any more.

BEN. Did I?

ANNA. Yeah. After your third pint of punch you really opened up. You said you felt stifled and that it's the Tories' fault and you've applied for a job at a film company.

BEN. A training scheme, yeah.

ANNA. Did you hear anything yet?

BEN. Not yet.

Pause.

ANNA. What's the company called again?

BEN. 'What's in a Name?'

ANNA. Very good. (*Beat.*) What's it called?

BEN. What's what called?

ANNA. The company.

BEN. 'What's in a Name?' That's what it's called.

ANNA. Oh.

BEN. Have you heard of it?

ANNA. No.

It's a good question though. *What's in a name?* What do you think of my name?

BEN. Anna.

ANNA. I know what it is. I said what do you think of it?

BEN. Yeah, it's alright.

ANNA. Can you imagine saying it?

BEN. What do you mean 'imagine saying it'? I can say it: Anna.

ANNA. No but like… a lot. Like over and over again. In a thousand different ways.

BEN. Oh you mean if we were like together?

ANNA. Sure.

BEN. As I said, I don't think –

ANNA. I know! I just mean, hypothetically.

BEN. Hypothetically… *Anna*. You know what, I guess I'd mainly call you 'baby' or something if we were together.

ANNA. Eugh.

BEN. What?

ANNA. Don't you dare call me that.

BEN. Why not?

ANNA. Because it's disgusting. People calling each other 'baby' is the worst.

BEN. What about, like, bespoke nicknames?

ANNA. Oh like cute, slightly coded, 'just between us' nicknames that a couple makes up for each other?

BEN. Yeah.

ANNA. That's even worse.

[*This section should be experimented with – actors to find nonsense words they like saying and stage a silly little make-believe dialogue between two soppy lovers, e.g.…*]

Like Shmoop. (*With mocking relish.*) P-p-pudge.

BEN. 'I call her Shmeep and she calls me Pups.'

ANNA. Shbee.

BEN. Mooshey. Bleeby.

She laughs. He finds a trainer.

ANNA. Do you know how to pronounce my surname?

BEN. Yeah!

ANNA. Go on then.

She begins pottering about, vaguely tidying up. Prepping for a shower.

BEN. Thingy. Kulcsh–

ANNA. No.

BEN. Well, I know how to spell it.

ANNA. Go on then.

BEN. K–U–L–S.

ANNA. No.

BEN. Well I know, like, what it looks like.

ANNA. What it looks like?

BEN. Yeah, as in I can visualise it.

ANNA. Oh my god. You know me so well.

BEN. Russian is a difficult language.

ANNA. It's not Russian.

BEN. What is it then?

ANNA. Polish. It's Kulczyński.

BEN. Are you Polish?

ANNA. No.

BEN. Are your parents?

ANNA. No.

BEN. Grandparents.

ANNA. Yeah, my granddad.

BEN. Cool.

ANNA. So I have got a bit of edge.

He laughs. He finds his other trainer. Starts putting it on.

I thought you wanted a shower.

BEN. I'm not allowed.

ANNA. You can go after me.

BEN. Nah.

ANNA. Are you joking? You're not gonna wash?

BEN. I'll shower at home.

ANNA. But you're all, y'know…

She gestures vaguely at his midriff.

BEN. I want to leave it marinating. So I can smell you. Smell your juices. Maybe have a sort of Proustian wank when I get home.

ANNA. Shut up!

BEN. Have you got any deodorant?

She chucks him a spray can of perfumed deodorant.

Don't you have a less… gendered one?

ANNA. No, sorry.

He sprays a cursory amount under each arm, grimacing.

You could leave a deodorant here maybe.

BEN. I'm hungry now actually. Do you wanna go for brunch?

ANNA. I thought you've a shitload of marking.

BEN. I can make time for a spot of brunch with a pretty young lady on a fresh spring morn.

He goes to touch her cheek delicately, taking the piss. She bats his hand away.

ANNA. Afternoon now.

BEN. Fuck. And it's Saturday innit. We'll probably have to wait ages for a table.

ANNA. Let's stay here. I'll make us lunch.

BEN thinks about it.

I've got lemon tart for after.

BEN. Really? Cos of me.

ANNA. Nah, I just fancied a lemon tart.

BEN. I can't believe you did that.

ANNA. I didn't do any– wait you stink!!

Sniffs his armpit.

Go and have a shower!!

BEN. No!

ANNA. Yes! If you don't have a shower you can't have lemon tart.

BEN. Fuck's sake.

He takes a towel from her. ANNA picks up another towel and follows him.

What are you doing?

ANNA (*off-handed*). I'm coming with you.

He smiles. They kiss and exit…

End of One.

Two

ANNA*'s bedroom. Night. Winter.* ANNA *wears* BEN*'s jumper and PJ bottoms.* BEN *in jeans and jumper.*

BEN *has just given* ANNA *flowers. They are in a pint glass of water.*

ANNA. Thank you for my lovely flowers.

And thank you for a lovely night. I had a really good time.

BEN. What was your favourite bit?

ANNA. Probably kissing you when the guy was playing 'Moon River'.

BEN. Over and over again!

ANNA. Do you think that's all he does, just stands by the river when the moon is out playing 'Moon River'?

BEN. Not a bad life.

She kisses him. He smiles. He kisses her back, becoming quickly quite vigorous. They move over to the bed. Gently he pushes her on to the bed and lies down next to her. They keep kissing. He pauses briefly to take things out of his pockets and then moves on top of her, becoming more vigorous still. For a few moments their passions amplify. BEN *begins trying to remove* ANNA*'s top. Then suddenly,* ANNA*'s not really into it.*

Alright?

She breaks away slightly.

ANNA. Yeah, sorry. I just remembered the washing.

BEN. What washing?

ANNA. In the machine. It'll smell.

BEN. So what?

ANNA. Most of it's your stuff.

BEN. I've got stuff in the drawer. Just… don't worry. You're always fixating else on something instead of being in the moment.

ANNA. It's just distracting me.

BEN *climbs back on to her. She laughs.*

BEN. The moment! The moment!

They start kissing again. She's more into it now. But then, fairly soon, she isn't.

You alright?

ANNA. Yeah… I'm… sorry.

BEN. Shall I get the washing?

ANNA. It's not the washing.

BEN. What is it then?

ANNA. I just. I dunno… I'm sorry. Just not very relaxed tonight.

BEN. Are you worried about your coil hurting?

ANNA. Maybe. Dunno.

BEN. Are you just bored of me?

ANNA. No! Of course I'm not! It just… sometimes happens. I'm just not in the mood, y'know.

BEN. Just not in the mood. Yeah, sure. Sorry.

ANNA. I'm sorry, Shbeen. I've just been feeling a bit tense.

BEN. Why are you tense?

ANNA. I dunno. Work stuff maybe.

Pause.

And maybe just not feeling very sexy at the moment maybe.

BEN. But you're not feeling less attracted to me?

ANNA. No.

She shakes her head. Distractedly, she begins moisturising.

BEN. Shall I go home?

ANNA. Why?!

BEN. Cos…

ANNA. Because we're not having sex?

BEN. Well…

ANNA. That's not what a relationship is. Only seeing each other to have sex. I promise I still find you attractive and it's just me being a bit tense at the moment and I really want you to stay.

He mumbles something.

What?

BEN. I said I'll stay.

ANNA. Good.

She kisses him. Gets up, starts sorting out work clothes, etc.

How would you get home at this time anyway?

BEN. I dunno, walk.

ANNA. I wouldn't let you walk at this time of night.

BEN. What do you mean you wouldn't let me?

ANNA. You wouldn't let me walk home from yours at this time, would you?

BEN. Well, I wouldn't stop you. But it's not the same for girls is it? Anyway, you wouldn't have to because we never stay at mine.

ANNA. Are you serious?

BEN. Nah, I'm just joking.

ANNA. Do you not think we stay at yours enough?

BEN. I didn't say anything about 'enough'. We just never stay at mine, which is fine.

ANNA. I'm sorry, it's just not great when the lights don't work and the washing machine's broken and the shower either burns you or freezes you to ice.

BEN. Well there's nothing I can do.

ANNA. Except for get it all fixed.

BEN. I don't have the money!

ANNA. Tell the landlord to pay.

BEN. I'm behind on the rent… (*Conceding.*) I'll get it sorted.

ANNA. Hmm. Oh god. I don't know what to wear for work.

BEN (*scoffing*). It's a hard life, innit.

ANNA. It is actually.

BEN. Yeah?

ANNA. Yeah. Well. Don't worry, it's boring.

BEN. What is?

ANNA. Just work stuff.

BEN. What about it?

ANNA. Oh I dunno. I just. Toni, left, the girl I told you about who's pregnant.

BEN *looks blank*.

Don't you remember?

BEN (*feigning?*). Oh yeah, I do, yeah.

ANNA. Well she went on extended maternity leave and I thought maybe I'd get her job or at least be asked to apply but they just did an external appointment.

BEN. Right.

ANNA. So yeah. Now, I'm just really feeling like I don't know what to do.

BEN. I thought you wanna be a psychologist or a psychotherapist.

ANNA. Yeah but I can't just wake up tomorrow and be a psychotherapist, can I?

BEN. Well yeah but you can wake up and apply for a course.

ANNA. It's not that simple.

BEN. Why not?

ANNA. I dunno. Just don't feel ready.

BEN. Well you're stuck then, aren't ya?

ANNA (*mock-woefully*). I guess I am.

She heads towards the door.

BEN. Where are you going?

ANNA. To clean my teeth. And the washing still needs doing.

He doesn't respond. She sighs quietly as she exits.

BEN ruminates, after a second he gets up and looks thoughtful. He looks in the mirror. Poses. Tries to look better. Maybe checks out his muscles and gut. He wanders back to the bed seeming a bit lost. Notices her phone. Furtively he looks at the door, sits on the bed, then picks up the phone, begins looking at it. After a few seconds he hears ANNA coming and chucks the phone back on the bed.

ANNA re-enters flossing her teeth.

You alright?

BEN. Uh-huh.

She looks a tad suspicious for a moment. BEN watches her, slightly sheepish. Pause. Now BEN sits looking pregnant with thought.

ANNA. You sure you're alright. Do you want to say something?

BEN. No. I was gonna say something earlier but the mood got… killed.

ANNA. What is it?

BEN. Doesn't matter.

She stops what she's doing.

ANNA (*genuine concern*). What is it?

BEN. It's nothing bad. Well, in a way it is.

ANNA. Ben!

BEN. I want to say… y'know.

Pause. He gestures for her to sit. She sits.

ANNA. What?!

BEN (*coyly*). The thing. A big thing.

ANNA. What thing?

He laughs. Embarrassed.

BEN. I don't wanna say it cos I'm gonna be in a vulnerable position. The power's gonna ch– well not the power but.

ANNA. Just fucking say it!

BEN (*looking at the ground*). I… love… you. I love ya.

He looks up. ANNA *says nothing. She looks mildly surprised and then mildly traumatised.* BEN *looks even more embarrassed now. He looks at her, tries to meet her eye. He pulls away slightly.*

Okay. It's … yeah. Is it something you feel? Do you want to say – Can you tell me ho– What's going on? What's going on in that *braaain* then?

ANNA. I want to.

BEN. But…

ANNA. No buts. Well. I want to *but* if I said it, I'd be lying. Not lying but…

BEN (*trying to sound really positive*). I get it. Don't worry.

ANNA. To say it you have to really mean it. And if I said it, I wouldn't mean it as much as I'd want to mean it. What do I mean? I mean, I mean do you mean it?

BEN. I do mean it. I wish I didn't mean it. That's not what
I mean. I mean – no fuck it. I mean it and I'm glad I mean it.

Pause.

ANNA. How long do you think you've… *felt* it?

BEN. I dunno. A month? Three months? Maybe since I met you.

It's weird because I had got to a stage in my life where I was
actually feeling alright. I made the decision I wanted to leave
teaching. I know how to manage my life a bit better. But
there was this sense of: wanting someone to share it with.
What's the point of if it's just for yourself. I guess I wanted
someone to make risotto for, y know?

ANNA. And that one risotto you made was great.

BEN. I've cooked other stuff for you!

ANNA. I know, I'm joking. Sorry, I interrupted.

BEN. Yeah, so and then I met you and you made me laugh.

ANNA. Did I?

BEN. Yeah.

ANNA (*slightly fishing for a compliment*). How?

BEN. At your housewarming. And then when we went to the
fair! We went on the shaking shack.

ANNA. Which was not shaky *in the slightest*.

BEN (*laughing*). Yeah yeah. And you were sort of taking the
piss out of it, like pretending to be shaking more than you
were, going: (*Acts it out, sarcastic voice.*) 'Ooh I'm really
shaking a lot here; I'm worried for my internal organs.'

ANNA. Well I'm sorry I had just paid two pounds to be in
a shaking shack that didn't shake. It was just a *normal shack*.
It was a *shuddering* shack at best.

BEN *finds this really funny.*

What? What? Ben!

BEN. Ah. I dunno! I just knew. At that moment. I was like: this woman. She's good. She's a good 'un. I realised that everything's been more *solid* of late, and that's down to you.

She kisses him. Smiles. Brushes his hair. After a moment, it's her turn to do a nice speech:

ANNA. I definitely feel that too. That everything's just been more… *vivid* since we've been together. I've never really met anyone like you. Someone so thoughtful and passionate and angry but sort of in a sensitive way. It's funny because I wasn't sure at first. And Caroline and – (*Halts on this thread, changes topic.*) but yeah you mean so much to me.

BEN. Wait, Caroline what?

ANNA. Nothin–

BEN. I knew Caroline had a problem with me.

ANNA. She doesn't have a problem with you. She likes you. I just told her about the flowers and she said it was incredibly cute.

BEN. 'Cute'?

ANNA. It's just when we first started going out. Caroline and some of my friends just were surprised because you weren't my usual type.

BEN. What, posh?

ANNA. Well yeah. I guess I just had narrow horizons. But now you've broadened them and I couldn't be happier.

BEN. But you're not gonna say 'I love you'?

She looks for a second like she might, but then says…

ANNA. No.

BEN. Right.

ANNA. Not no, as in 'never'. Just not tonight. (*And then, more softly.*) I feel so much for you, Shbeen. *So much.*

He waits for her to say more. She doesn't.

BEN. Well. That's something.

She gets up and begins getting ready for bed.

ANNA. It's late.

BEN. It's not that late.

ANNA. It is. 11.37.

BEN. I'm not tired enough to sleep yet.

ANNA. You're only not tired because you stay up until 3 a.m. for no reason.

BEN. I'm on half-term!

ANNA. But even during term-time you stay up late, and if you've been drinking or whatever.

BEN. Have you got a problem with me drinking?

ANNA. No, I'm just saying, if you got up early you could get on with applying for jobs and internships and stuff.

BEN *(muttered)*. Good idea.

ANNA. I told you you should ask Seb if there's anything going at his company.

BEN. I don't wanna work there.

ANNA. Why not?

BEN. I just don't.

Pause. BEN *sits on edge of bed, looking troubled.*

ANNA. What's wrong?

BEN. Nothing. I really want a cigarette.

ANNA. Oh fuck, the fucking washing!

She rubs her temples. She moves to the door, then stops and looks at him. He doesn't move.

Ben, sorry to be a bitch but just cos it's mainly your stuff, would you mind hanging the washing?

BEN. Oh yeah sure, you should have just said.

She bites her tongue.

ANNA. Thanks.

He exits. Sleepily she looks at herself in the mirror. She looks tired, a bit glum. Assesses her body, pinches at her belly. She moves over to the bed. Picks up his phone, keys and wallet and places them on the bedside table. She gets into bed and begins to drift off.

BEN *returns with the washing.*

BEN. I really fucking want a cig, man!

He dumps the washing and notices ANNA *is drifting off.*

ANNA. Can you turn the main light off?

BEN. Wait, aren't you waiting for me?

ANNA. Waiting for you to what?

BEN. Go to sleep.

ANNA. We don't need to go to sleep at exactly the same second.

BEN (*self-pitying*). Right. Night then.

He begins hanging the washing.

ANNA. Come here…

BEN *goes over to the bed. She takes his arm, moves her towards him. He kneels on the bed. They kiss.*

Goodnight. Shbeen. Sorry I'm in a shitty mood.

BEN. It's alright. I just wanna make you happy.

ANNA. You do make me happy. Thank you for my lovely flowers.

BEN. That's alright, Wannna. I love you.

She smiles and lowers her head to the pillow. He stands looking at her poignantly.

ANNA (*sleepy mumbling*). Canyaturrn lightoff?

BEN. Yeah sorry.

He turns the main light off. Just lamplight now. He looks around for occupation. Goes to the bed and picks up the laptop. Opens it and starts browsing.

ANNA. How long you will be?

BEN. With what?

ANNA. The washing.

BEN. I'll do it in a sec. I'm just reading an article about vertical farming.

She jumps up.

ANNA. I'll do it.

BEN. Why? I said I'll do it in a sec.

ANNA. I need the light off, Ben. Sorry.

BEN. Alright, I'll help.

He gets up and they both start hanging the clothes to dry. Her quickly, him less so.

ANNA. Make sure you don't scrunch them up or they won't dry.

BEN. Yes, boss.

He smiles. She doesn't smile back.

Sorry.

The washing hung up, she gets back into bed.

ANNA. Are you getting ready for bed?

BEN. Yeah, I guess.

He takes his jeans off and chucks them on the ground. He is now ready for bed.

ANNA. Will you turn the lamp off?

BEN. Sure.

He does so. Just the laptop lights the room now. He gets on to the bed to kiss her cheek.

Goodnight.

ANNA. Goodnight.

He sits up in bed looking a bit lost. After a moment, he picks up the laptop and continues browsing, illuminated by blue-ish light as ANNA *sleeps next to him.*

Slow fade to black.

End of Two.

Three

ANNA*'s room. Summer. A hot day.* BEN *sits with the laptop, concentrating.* ANNA *lolls about, bored.*

ANNA. I don't know what to do!

> *She gets up. Kicks around the room a bit. Wanders over to* BEN. *Rubs his head, flirts with him like a cat seeking attention. He doesn't break his concentration.*

I love you… Shbeen. Breeeen. Baby!

> *Her flirtation becomes more mischievous, almost violent. She tries to slide to nudge the laptop away from him.*

BEN (*abrupt, angry*). What are you doing?

ANNA (*mock-childishly*). I'm boooored.

BEN. I'm trying to concentrate. Do you not want to go on holiday?

ANNA. I want to do something today. It's so niiiiiiiiiice.

BEN. I thought we were booking a holiday.

ANNA. We can do that any time.

BEN (*severely*). But we just keep saying that and we just never end up going!

ANNA (*amused at his severity*). Sorry.

BEN. Where do *you* want to go on holiday?

ANNA. Don't mind.

BEN. Paris.

ANNA. No, not Paris.

BEN. Right. Where then?

ANNA. Don't mind. Just not Paris. Maybe we could to go Whitstable or somewhere.

BEN. I don't mean Whitstable, I mean a proper holiday. Somewhere different. For, like, a week, two weeks.

ANNA. You'll just get bored though.

BEN. Don't tell me how I'm gonna feel!

ANNA. Sorry, baby. Don't get stressed. I know you're hungover.

BEN. I'm not hungover! It's just nicotine withdrawal.

ANNA. Yes, sorry. You're doing really well.

Still standing up, she hugs his head, comforting him. He puts an arm round her.

It's so hot today. We should go to the park. Let's get a lemon tart and eat it in the park!

BEN *laughs, slightly dismissively.*

What?

BEN. Nothing.

ANNA. Tell me!

BEN. Just… can you never think of anything to do except eat lemon tart?

She lets go of him, steps back.

ANNA. What do you mean?

BEN. I mean a relationship shouldn't be mediated through consumption.

ANNA. 'Mediated through consumption'?

BEN. Modern couples. Modern people in general. Can we not fucking interact with each other any more, without having to buy some arbitrary meaningless product? (*Mocking voices.*) 'Ooh we love lemon tart, that's our thing.' 'We like going out for Prosecco – he didn't like it before I met him, but he loves it now.' 'We just bought a coffee machine.' 'We just bought a spiraliser.' 'We just bought a NutriBullet.' 'Quick let's check the weekend supplements, find out what clothes to buy and music to pretend to like and which new fucking jam-jar cocktail bar we should waste our money in this month, lest we have to just stay in our tiny shitty flat full of kitsch overpriced shit from made.com because Ikea's really basic… and have to actually fucking talk to each other.'

Pause.

ANNA. Good stuff. What have you been reading?

BEN. What do you mean?

ANNA. Like a Frankie Boyle column in the *Guardian* or…?

BEN. Why do I need to have been reading something?

ANNA. You just seem really *inspired*. By *something*.

During BEN*'s explanation,* ANNA *looks exaggeratedly bored.*

BEN. It's just I'm not saying this is my opinion, but there is an argument, that because the old rituals and conventions of love have been jettisoned, capitalism produces new erm modes, new ways of expressing love, and in the modern capitalist society, we're alienated from our selfhoods and from other people, so love can only be mediated through consumption.

ANNA. Right. Erm. So if that's not your opinion, what is it?

BEN (*faux-offhand*). I dunno, I was talking to my friend Gillian about her PHD.

ANNA. Oh your '*friend* Gillian'?

BEN *just looks at her. She smiles back. She shrugs. She sits down.*

BEN. What do you mean?

ANNA. It's just funny how you always say 'my friend Gillian'. You wouldn't preface anyone else's name with 'my friend'. I wouldn't say, y'know, 'my friend Seb has made a new documentary about the Croatian far right' or whatever I'd just say 'Seb' has done it.

Pause. Bit of a stand-off.

BEN. Right. It's just cos I know you don't know Gillian that well, because she's my uni friend. Just putting her into context.

ANNA. Thank you. She's in context for me now so thanks for that.

BEN. Look I don't know if you think something's going on with me and Gillian.

ANNA. Oh my god, Ben! No, I don't. Can we just stop talking about Gillian?

BEN. Okay. Sorry.

Pause.

ANNA. Is booking a holiday mediating love through consumption?

BEN. That's different.

ANNA. How?

BEN. Because that's about the place, it's…

ANNA. It still costs money. It's still a consumer product, a commodity advertised to us.

BEN. Yes but, it doesn't matter.

He does a 'amusedly disagreeing' face.

ANNA. Don't do that.

BEN. Do what?

ANNA. That face when I make a point and you don't agree with it and you just laugh like 'it's not even worth me explaining why you're wrong'.

He does the face again.

You're doing it aga–

He breaks into a smile. ANNA *registers that's he's joking.*

You wanker!

She backhands him playfully.

BEN. Oi.

He takes her hands, as if to waltz.

You're right. Holidays are just… consumerist frivolities.

ANNA. I didn't say that!

BEN. No. But. Yeah. Hypocritical.

Pause. Sighs. They share a look of mutual contrition.
BEN *embraces her.*

ANNA. So how can we mediate our love if not through commerce?

BEN *smiles, rising to the challenge. Commandingly, silently, he takes* ANNA *by the shoulders and repositions her, makes her stand still. He takes the laptop – puts on some upbeat music. Takes* ANNA *by the hands, dances. She laughs, genuinely shy. Tries to bat him away. His conviction overwhelms her.*

You know that YouTube is a commercial medium, don't you? Music is a commercial medium.

BEN. Music is the food of love.

ANNA. Food is a commercial medium so love is a commercial medium.

BEN *says nothing, keeps dancing. Spins her around, she joins in – reluctantly at first, and then more spiritedly. They're really going for it.*

BEN *tries to lift* ANNA *up.*

No!

He keeps trying.

Ben!

Manages to lift her.

I'm serious! Put me down!

Losing grip, lacking strength, HE DROPS HER! She hits the ground roughly, hard.

Ow!

BEN. I'm sorry!

ANNA. You fucking wanker!

BEN. I'm really sorry! Are you okay?

He shuts the laptop, turning the music off. Crouches down to her, she turns away. She clutches the small of her back.

Are you alright?

ANNA. That fucking hurt!

BEN. Is it your back?

ANNA. I told you to put me down. You're not strong enough.

BEN. Let me see.

ANNA. Get off.

He manages to take a look at her back.

BEN. You've grazed it.

ANNA. *You've* grazed it, you fucking cunt.

BEN. I'm really sorry.

ANNA. Go get the fucking Savlon.

BEN. What's Savlon?

ANNA. Oh my god!

She gets up and moves to the door. He blocks her way.

BEN. Sit down! Let me go. It's cream right? Is it in the bathroom?

ANNA. In the bathroom cabinet.

BEN. I'll go. Sit down.

She sits down. Picks up her phone. Increases her wincing as she hears BEN *return. He returns with the Savlon. Holds it out.*

Here you go.

ANNA. You put it on.

BEN. Yes.

He kneels down. She leans forward. He lifts her T-shirt at the back.

ANNA. Ouch!

BEN. Sorry!

ANNA. I'll do it.

BEN. No, let me.

ANNA. Fucking hurts.

BEN. I'm really sorry.

ANNA. Yeah you said.

Silence. Then BEN*'s phone starts ringing. He doesn't react. Just keeps rubbing the cream in.*

You gonna get that.

BEN. Nah.

ANNA. Get it. It's annoying me.

He gets up. Looks at his phone. Cancels the call.

Who was it?

BEN. Just Amir.

ANNA. Why didn't you answer it?

BEN. Cos I'm doing the cream.

ANNA. Ring him back.

BEN. I will in a bit. We're hanging out later, he'll just be ringing about that.

ANNA. Are you?

BEN. Yeah.

ANNA. Why didn't you tell me?

BEN. I thought I did. Why, is it a problem? (*Beat*.) Why?

ANNA. No. I just thought we were gonna do something tonight.

BEN. Oh okay. Didn't realise, but that's fine. Sorry, I'll cancel.

ANNA. Don't be stupid. Call him back.

BEN. No I'm doing the cream.

ANNA. No just leave it now. Thank you.

BEN. What are you doing?

ANNA. I'm texting Caroline. If you're meeting Amir.

BEN. I just said I'll cancel.

ANNA. Honestly, baby, it's fine. I'll just see where Caroline is and –

She notices a new text.

Oh she's busy. Thass annoyin'!

BEN. What's she doing?

ANNA. She's going to one of her feminism things. Workshop things.

BEN. Oh yeah. They sound interesting.

ANNA. They sound mad. (*Tuts*.) I wanted to talk to her.

BEN. What about?

ANNA. Just boring stuff. (*Slightly ironic tone*.) Just work stuff.

He moves towards her – slightly pitifully.

BEN. You can talk to me about work stuff.

She gives him a patronising pat.

ANNA. I know, baby.

BEN. Why do you feel you can talk to Caroline and not me about work stuff?

ANNA. You said it's boring. I don't mind, it is boring. We can't all quit our jobs and become private tutors.

BEN. I haven't become a private tutor. I've – I've. I'm just tutoring until my internship starts.

ANNA. Sorry, yeah that's what I meant.

BEN. Anyway, I never said your job is boring.

ANNA. Yes you did.

BEN. When?

ANNA. A few weeks ago. We were on the bus in the morning. I was going to work. You were going home to sit around wanking all day or whatever it is you do now.

BEN. I don't sit around w–

ANNA *starts texting. Looks up intermittently.*

ANNA. I'm joking! We were going past the library and I said 'I don't want to go to work today.' I said 'I wish I could go and sit in the library all day and read and work out what I'm gonna do with my life.' And you said 'You need to find a less boring job then you wouldn't get that yearning.'

BEN. I don't think I did say that.

ANNA. Yes you did. Exact words.

BEN. I wouldn't have said 'less boring'. I think said 'more meaningful'.

ANNA. So you think my life is meaningless?

BEN. Everyone's life is meaningless.

ANNA. No it isn't.

BEN. Yes it is.

ANNA. No it isn't.

BEN. Yes it is.

ANNA, *having finished texting, gets up and starts doing her make-up in the mirror.*

ANNA. Is your life meaningless?

BEN. Of course.

ANNA. Wow, thanks a lot.

BEN. What?

ANNA. You said your life is meaningless. So do I not give your life meaning?

BEN. Of course. I didn't mean meaningless in an everyday, 'life is shit, I've got no reason to get out of bed' way. I meant in a grand, existential, 'the cosmos is indifferent to us, we will die and be forgotten and leave no imprint on eternity' way. And it's terrifying. Sometimes. But, y'know, you are the best distraction, the best comfort, in the face of all that meaninglessness that I'll ever need.

Pause. A calmness between them suddenly. She steps away from the mirror, towards him.

ANNA. I'm so glad I've got you.

She hugs him, cheek against his chest.

BEN. I'm so glad I've got you.

ANNA. It hurts when you leave me, it feels cold.

BEN. I'm not gonna leave you!

ANNA. I mean just when you leave the house, when you leave the room even. Every time you go out of the door, I feel like… like… someone's just stolen five hundred pounds from my bank account.

BEN. I'll stay in tonight.

ANNA. Don't be stupid. It's just weird, it's silly. Do you get that?

BEN. Yeah I do.

ANNA. What am I gonna do?

BEN. Tonight?

ANNA. Ever.

BEN. Well maybe you should look more at psychology courses.

ANNA. That's what my mum keeps telling me as well. She says my dad'll pay for it.

BEN. Oh so your mum and I don't disagree on everything then.

ANNA. What's that supposed to mean?

BEN. We didn't find much to agree on the other week, did we?

ANNA. I told you not to worry about that. First meetings are stressful. Maybe you shouldn't have started talking about 'the wealth gap'.

BEN. Well maybe she shouldn't have started talking about 'immigration'.

ANNA. I told you my dad said you were 'principled'.

BEN. He didn't like my principles though, did he?

ANNA. No.

BEN. Do you think they like me?

Pause.

ANNA. Well I don't think they will when I tell them what you did to my back.

BEN. That was an accident!

ANNA. I'm kidding!

Hits him playfully. Then hugs him.

I'm going out.

BEN. What? Where?

ANNA. I'm gonna go to this workshop with Caroline. Beats sitting around here on my own.

BEN. Do you want me to cance–

ANNA (*firmly*). Honestly. Ben. No. I'm sure this thing will
be… (*Bit tongue-in-cheek*.) very enlightening. When are you
meeting Amir?

BEN. In an hour or so. Do you mind if I wait here till then?

ANNA. You don't need to ask.

BEN. Taaa.

ANNA. You like it here don't you? It is because your flat is
a fucking nightmare.

BEN. I'm gonna get it all sorted! I'll get loads of new clients in
September and do it then.

ANNA. You start your internship in September.

BEN. But I can tutor in the evenings and weekends. And the
internship's only for six weeks.

ANNA. Reckon they'll give you a job at the end?

BEN. I dunno, man. I was thinking maybe I don't wanna work
in film anyway.

This is news to ANNA.

ANNA. Why not?

BEN. I dunno, there's just maybe other stuff I wanna do instead.
I think I wanna learn to code.

ANNA (*very surprised*). You want to learn to code?

BEN. Yeah, or do an MA maybe. Let's just see how the
internship goes first.

ANNA. Right. Yeah.

Bit of a pause.

BEN. I'm sorry I was a dick.

ANNA. You weren't.

BEN. But we got like, testy. I don't like arguing.

ANNA. Nor do I.

She kisses him.

BEN. We should go on holiday.

ANNA. Yes we should. Let's book something tomorrow.

BEN. Great.

ANNA. I've gotta go. The patriarchy won't bring itself down.

BEN (*correcting*). 'Bring *down itself*.'

ANNA. What?

BEN (*cheeky*). You ended a sentence on a preposition.

ANNA (*ironic, sassy*). Erm, don't mansplain to me please!

They both chuckle.

BEN. I love you.

ANNA. I love you.

They kiss, meaningfully.

I'll call you later.

BEN. Have a good night.

She picks up her bag and coat.

ANNA. You too. Don't drink too much.

BEN (*laughing, self-deprecating*). I won't.

Exits. BEN *watches after her. Looks sad a second. Looks around the room. Slightly anguished. Sits down. Looks a bit lost. Remembering something, grabs his phone. Calls someone.*

(*Into phone*). Alright, buddy. Sorry I missed your call. Still up for a drink in a bit? Oh okay. Wait, is this the dancer? A barrister! (*Laughs.*) You're doing alright for yourself at the moment, aren't you? No, no worries, man. Good luck.

He hangs up, a bit disappointed. He seems at a loss for a moment as to what to do next. Then, slightly shiftily he picks up his phone, agonises for a moment, before making another call.

(*Into phone*.) Hey, Gillian, how are you? Yeah, not bad. Do you wanna go for a drink tonight maybe?

End of Three.

Four

ANNA*'s room. Night. There is now a large, Scotch-bonnet-type shell on the shelf.*

Thumping music, and crowd noise – there is a party in the house. We sit with this, the room empty, for a while. Then ANNA *and* BEN *burst in. They are both dressed up for a party* (BEN *more casual than smart-casual*).

BEN*'s knuckles are bleeding.* ANNA *is concerned, confused, breathless. She shuts the door behind them.*

ANNA. What the fuck, Ben? Let me see your hand. (*Looks.*) Oh my god. It's bleeding!

BEN. Yeah I know it's fucking bleeding!

ANNA. Why the hell did you punch the wall?

BEN. It was either the wall or someone's face.

ANNA. Whose face? Seb's?

BEN. How did you guess?

ANNA. Why would you want to punch Seb?

BEN. Oh don't take the piss! You know full fucking well why and you're deliberately fucking winding me up saying you don't.

His anger rises and he moves as if to punch the wall again. ANNA *grabs him.*

ANNA. Ben, just calm down! Sit down, okay?

She sits him on the bed. Grabs a tissue.

Let me clean the blood.

She tends to his knuckles.

Really, Ben, I'm not trying to be antagonistic, I just don't understand what's wrong. It's something Seb did or I did, but you need to explain it.

BEN. It shouldn't need explaining. You were just…

He is too enervated to articulate the problem.

ANNA. Just what?

BEN.…dancing.

ANNA. So what?

BEN. You never dance.

ANNA. I'm a bit drunk! It's nearly Christmas. Can't I have a dance?

BEN. It was the way you were dancing. Like all in sync with each other. And the way you were looking at each other.

ANNA. How were we looking at each other?

BEN. Like in each other's eyes.

ANNA. People tend to look at each other's eyes when they interact!

BEN. Nah, but it was the way you were looking into each other's eyes.

ANNA. What '*way*'?

BEN. Like…

Tries to recreate it – widens his eyes as if staring into someone else's and smiles and moves his head a bit.

ANNA. What's the hell is that?

He does it again with a bit more vigour. She stands up.

I've just got no idea what that's supposed to be. Look, Ben. I understand. Maybe I was flirting with Seb a bit but he's an old friend and we were just messing about and you've really overreacted. I dunno what your problem is with Seb. He likes you. He keeps offering you running work for fuck's sake.

BEN. How many times have I gotta tell you? I don't want to do fucking running work for fucking Seb.

ANNA. Why not?

He stands up.

BEN. Because it would be humiliating okay? That's the truth. It's patronising that he keeps saying he'll give me some shitty low-status job even though he's younger than me. He's just doing it to belittle me and impress you. And I know you think I should set my ego aside and just take it because I didn't get a job from my internship and why was I even doing internships when I'm twenty-nine and I'm just treading water but I can't fucking do it! I can't fucking do it and I'm getting worked up again because just thinking about you and him makes me angry and I'm sorry.

Pause as she takes this in.

ANNA. Well, I didn't realise you felt like that. And I'm sorry you feel like that. But it's really no excuse to make a scene. Everyone was watching.

BEN. I'm sorry. I don't why I acted like that. I just felt possessed. Look we're both drunk. Let's just sit down and return to normality.

He sits. She remains standing. She looks more anguished now.

ANNA. I don't really know what normality is, Ben.

BEN. What do you mean?

ANNA. I just feel weeeird.

BEN. Oh. Do you want some water or something? Someone might have a Valium?

ANNA. No, not weird like that. (*Pause.*) Not micro-weird, macro-weird.

BEN. What do you mean?

Pause.

ANNA. I mean do you feel like things have been weird for a while? Different y'know.

BEN. Different from what?

ANNA. I dunno. Maybe now isn't the right time to start talking about it. Here have some Savlon.

She moves to put Savlon on his knuckles. He doesn't let her.

BEN. No, Anna, what? Start talking about what?

ANNA. I I I just I dunno. I dunno.

BEN. Say what you wanna say.

ANNA. I dunno what I wanna say. I wanna say something and I don't know what it is. I'm just speaking and I don't really know what I wanted to say. I didn't have any intention of saying this at all and suddenly I'm saying… (*Breaks off.*)

BEN. What are you saying?

ANNA (*almost marvelling at herself, like she's outside of herself*). I'm talking like there's a problem… like we're gonna…

BEN. What?

She looks gravely at him.

Break up!? No. (*Calmly convincing, almost laughing.*) No. We're not. Of course we're not.

ANNA. No. I mean I don't want that. But for some reason I'm saying. I'm like I dunno what is this, a warning? Not a warning a… we gotta… things aren't right, are they?

BEN. No. (*Beat.*) What do you mean?

ANNA. Because… we both seem like we're not making each other very happy at the moment. You wouldn't have punched a wall if you were happy, would you?

Distracted, unable to look at him, she picks up the shell on the shelf and inspects it.

BEN. Well you can't be happy all the time.

ANNA. No, but –

BEN. I know I acted like a madman but it's just because of how much I love you. And cos I'm pissed and maybe because I'm a bit insecure. Are you saying you're not happy?

ANNA. I dunno. I've sort of forgotten what the normal way to feel is. I know I'm not as happy as I was.

BEN. As you were when? You mean the beginning of the relationship? Cos you're not gonna be that happy forev–

ANNA. No even later than that. Like – (*Plucks example out of air.*) like when we went to Whitstable. I couldn't imagine ever being happier than that.

They both smile. Reflective pause.

BEN (*indicating the shell*). Can you hear the sea in it?

She chuckles and cursorily puts it to her ear.

ANNA. No.

BEN. Give it here.

She hands it him. He puts it to his here. Listens, concentrating for a moment.

I can. I can hear the sea!

She manages a laugh.

ANNA. No, you can't.

BEN. I can hear that day.

ANNA. What do you mean you can hear that day?

BEN. I can. I can hear us walking round those gardens. I can hear that brass band playing. I can hear you having a pickled egg. I can hear you not giving me any of your fucking pickled egg.

ANNA. I think you'll hear me giving you a little bit if you listen properly. Can you hear us having a crab?

BEN. Yes, I can hear us having a crab! (*Taking shell away from ear.*) Fuck! Do you remember that meal? (*Rushing towards her, urgently.*) Do you remember how good that was? The chips and the... what else?

ANNA (*shrinking back, amused and scared*). Mixed vegetables.

BEN. Fucking hell! The mixed vegetables. Do you remember that?

ANNA. Yes, Ben, I remember.

He stands up, returns shell to his ear.

It was a good day.

BEN. It was the best day of my life.

ANNA (*scoffing*). Shut up.

BEN. I'm not kidding. I can hear it. I can hear the best day of my life. I can hear us sitting on that beach. And I remember thinking, like, usually the sea freaks me out. You know people say the sea is calming. For me it's empty and vast, and unremitting, and grey. But sitting with you transformed the sea. It wasn't just calming… but meaningful, every wave was bestowing something, carrying meaning and, like, positivity. And I realised that that was down to you. Cos that's what love is, the power of another person to bestow meaning on to things, to almost transform things, the sea, the beach, the grey boring streets between my house and yours, a… fucking lemon tart. And you've still got that power, to render everything worth encountering, just by existing, just by being next to me. And – (*Begins choking up a bit.*) it devastates me to think that you're feeling like I can't do that for you any more.

He collects himself. She looks at him, trying to say something. She says nothing.

What are you thinking?

She takes the shell.

ANNA. It was a really good day. I remember you telling me something on the beach, that was really… wise.

BEN. What did I say?

ANNA. I don't remember.

Pause.

Something about the sea.

Pause.

BEN. Right.

ANNA. Something about the way we notice waves but we don't notice the tide and that's like life. It can feel like in life is just monotonous and nothing is changing but slowly through that monotonous repetition we're getting closer to where we need to be.

Pause.

BEN (*ironic*). That is clever.

ANNA. It was a long time ago! I just remember the sense of it. How it made me feel.

BEN. How did it make you feel?

ANNA. It made Sunday night, feel like a Saturday night.

BEN (*laughing a little bit*). That's nice. And how does this Saturday night feel?

ANNA. Hmm, like a Thursday night.

BEN. Yeah I was thinking that!

Pause.

(*Suddenly quite serious.*) I don't want to do this any more.

ANNA. Do what?

BEN. Getting fucked every weekend. Acting like a prick.

ANNA. You don't do it every weekend.

BEN. It feels like it. Ruining the Sunday. Feeling like shit until Wednesday and then only getting by on the anticipation of getting fucked again.

ANNA. Is that really how you feel?

BEN. I just don't need to do it any more. I just want to stay in, just me and you on a Saturday. Watch a film. Watch shitty TV. Spend two hours cooking one meal. Talk. Maybe a glass of wine. Maybe two glasses!

She laughs.

Wake up on Sunday. Go to a museum. Go for brunch. Go running or swimming or cycling.

She seems enticed by the idea, if a bit distrustful.

ANNA. But you hate all that, don't you? 'Smug-couple Sundays.'

BEN. I don't know! Maybe I don't. Maybe I was only hating it because I was seeing it from the outside. Trying to politicise it, saying it was bourgeois, or whatever where actually it was jealousy. Now I'm in it, I just see that it's enough. Love is enough.

Pause.

ANNA. Well yeah, but you've got to be happy.

BEN. Well yeah, but. I just hated couples and y'know 'fashionable' or modish ways of spending time together as a couple because I didn't have love. And. And. But the way I'm living isn't political or ideological or poetic, it's just immature. I'll be thirty next year for fuck's sake. I just need to grow up, stop doing drugs, quit smoking. Stay in at the weekend with you. Cook. Buy some art.

ANNA. We can't afford art.

BEN. Affordable art.

ANNA. We can't afford affordable art.

BEN. I'm just saying that that's what I want. That life with you. Not to be punching walls. Chatting shit at parties. Railing against stuff I don't have the power to change.

ANNA. I think it's just a weird time. In a lot of ways.

She checks her appearance in the mirror. He wanders over. Embraces her from behind. She smiles. Like this, they regard themselves in the mirror.

BEN. What do you think's going to happen?

ANNA. What do you mean?

BEN. With us?

ANNA. I don't know.

BEN. Shall we go back downstairs?

She doesn't answer but kisses him softly, tenderly. Suddenly, taken with new desire, she pushes him towards the bed, breaking off only to turn the light off and climb on top of him.

End of Four.

Five

BEN*'s empty bedroom. Night. We sit with the empty room for a little while, lit by a lamp. Then, from the hallway we hear a door open.* BEN *and* ANNA*'s voices are heard. They enter in winter-wear.* BEN *is wearing a Santa hat.* BEN *first then* ANNA*, he casually, she with a greater sense of occasion, almost trepidation.*

In as minimal but clear a way as possible the room needs to be differentiated from ANNA*'s. On the shelf is a deodorant, like the one from Scene One.*

ANNA. Hello, this room.

    BEN *laughs. He lifts up the duvet on the bed and flaps it up and down* (*like a mouth*).

BEN. Hello, Anna. I've missed you, even though you hardly ever came to visit me.

ANNA (*to the duvet, joining in with the riff*). Quiet, you!

    She gives the duvet a punitive slap.

Have you changed your sheets since I was last here.

BEN. Yeah loadsa times!

    She notices the deodorant on the shelf.

ANNA. Wait, is that mine?

BEN. Obviously.

    BEN *takes his coat off.*

ANNA. Why are you taking your coat off?

BEN. I'm hot.

ANNA. But we're not staying. I've gotta go.

BEN. Yeah, I'll only be a minute. I'll get the bus with you.

He starts looking round for something.

ANNA. I thought you were packed.

BEN. I am. Pretty much. Just need to grab a few more bits.

He starts chucking some stuff into an empty bag.

My mum told me to wish you happy Christmas by the way.

ANNA. Aw, wish her one from me.

BEN. She said you're very welcome to come and visit if you want.

ANNA. That's sweet.

BEN. When are you going home?

ANNA. Tomorrow. Getting a lift with my brother.

BEN. And what's this thing tonight?

ANNA. Caroline's engagement drinks.

BEN. I thought that was last night.

ANNA. No that was Florence's engagement drinks.

BEN. *Everyone*'s getting engaged.

ANNA. Yeah it's mad.

BEN. And how's the new flat?

ANNA. It's okay. Not as nice as the other one. And it's weird living with strangers but yeah – (*Mock-formal.*) a mature step towards adulthood.

He stops packing and looks thoughtful.

Ben, I'm gonna be late.

BEN. Weren't in such a rush when you were ordering another large wine were you?

ANNA. I thought we were going to talk.

BEN. We did talk. We talked for two hours!

ANNA. Not really.

> BEN *says nothing. Starts packing again.*

> We just reminisced for like an hour. And then talked about Adele for half an hour.

BEN. Fuck! I hardly even asked you how the MA's going?

ANNA. I told you, it's not an MA. (*Mock-formal.*) *It's* a part-time foundation certificate in counselling and psychotherapy. It's good. It's hard, especially as I'm still working but I feel like I'm on the right path. How about you? Are you looking forward to teaching again?

BEN. Yeah. Yeah it'll be good to teach real kids again. Not just millionaire-spawn. Will be a bit weird going back in at the deep end in January. But yeah. Exciting. And Gillian and I are gonna make a short film as well so…

ANNA. Cool.

BEN. So is this what you meant by talking?

ANNA. Erm. Maybe. I mean it's good to catch up but we sort of had a… purpose… for talking didn't we?

> *He doesn't look at her. Pretends to be looking for something.*

BEN. Well, shall we get to it now?

ANNA. There's no time now. You've got to get the train.

BEN. I've got an open ticket.

ANNA. I've got to get to Caroline's.

BEN. Well let's not go into the Christmas break with things up in the air.

ANNA. You sound like a football manager.

BEN. We gotta talk. Let's talk. Talk.

ANNA. Okay.

BEN. Sit down, take your coat off.

She sits down, doesn't take her coat off. He turns on the main light.

So what d–

ANNA. You got the light fixed.

BEN. Yep. Water had leaked into the circuit so they had to rerig all the wiring – Boring. Anyway erm look I. Yes. I know we need to talk. (*Inhales.*) But. I. Don't. Know – What is it exactly we need to talk about. Like… the future?

ANNA (*suddenly a bit unsure of herself*). Erm. Yeah. I guess we need… clarity.

BEN. Yeah. So how do we achieve clarity?

ANNA. I don't know.

BEN. How about – okay, how about we both talk about – (*Every word seems like a struggle but one he takes on doggedly.*) how things have been… and… how we've… Felt since… the 'break-up'. Erm yeah.

ANNA. Good idea.

BEN. Okay. Shall I go first?

ANNA. Okay.

BEN. So… when we broke up I know there was that tension between us that had just become too much, but I soon began to feel like I should have put up more resistance because… maybe your wanting to break up was, like, a test of the relationship…

She looks confused.

… as in, to test my, like, devotion.

Pause. He looks to her for assurance. She gives none.

I just feel that you've been as present and as constant and as complete a part of me since we stopped seeing each other as you were before. Which makes me think that tension was maybe quite contextual. But the love, basically, is pretty… essential. Yeah that's… yeah… my take.

He chortles. She chortles too.

Erm. Yeah. Your turn!

ANNA. Okay. I feel the same. In lots of ways. I miss you tremendously. And you're still absolutely part of me. And you always will be. And it's a sign of how good we were together that we've kept seeing each other. But we haven't really been together. We haven't… slept together for a while or anything. So the relationship has changed in a way.

BEN. Right. Yeah. It's ambiguous, right? Like what we are now. So I guess we need more definition over what the relationship is.

ANNA. How do we do that?

BEN. Like I said…

ANNA. Go on some dates…

BEN. Go on some dates. Like proper romantic dates, like make a real effort. To almost get to know each other all over again.

ANNA. Go back to the beginning?

BEN. Well. Yeah.

Pause.

Well not go back to the beginning. Well yes, go back to the beginning. Why not? Life is all about going back to the beginning. There are only four seasons coming round over and over again but when the daffodils bloom in the spring you don't go 'oh these yellow fuckers again!' That's just what life is. Resetting. Over and over again. And I want to reset over and over again with you!

ANNA (*after a moment's serious reflection*). 'Reset' kind of makes the relationship sound like a wifi router.

They both chuckle a bit.

BEN. You know what I mean.

ANNA. And when the tension comes back? We just buy a lemon tart and hope it goes away?

BEN. Yes… No… There's always tension. That's what life is. It can't always be summer. But with each season something does change. With each argument, and with each tricky week or whatever we learn better how to not let that tension get the better of us. Because I've never met anybody else I want to go on those fucking… cycles with. And I promise you won't find anybody who wants to go on that journey with you as much as I do.

She looks searchingly into his eyes. Very tentatively they kiss. She pulls away, seeming to regret her impulsivity.

Erm. I got you a Christmas present.

He gets up and takes a nicely wrapped gift from the corner.

ANNA. Oh.

BEN. Kinda why I asked you back. Didn't want to bring it to the pub.

He hands it to her.

ANNA. Oh my gosh.

She unwraps it. It's a poster for the Polish film version of To Kill a Mockingbird.

It's… what is it?

BEN. Well, so *Zabic* is 'to kill'. And I think *Drozda* is 'thrush'. Maybe they don't have mockingbirds in Poland.

ANNA. Oh my god, Ben.

BEN. Do you like it?

ANNA. I really like it.

BEN. I thought you might need some stuff to decorate your new room.

ANNA (*fighting tears*). I do. Thank you.

Impulsively, she holds him tight. Both seem to be tearing up slightly.

Do you have a cigarette?

BEN. No I've quit. Three months nearly.

ANNA. Wow. Well done. Do you have a tissue then?

BEN. Yeah. I'll get some toilet roll.

He stands up.

ANNA. No, wait. Got some in my bag.

She points to her handbag by the door.

Aloe vera.

They both laugh, snottily.

BEN. Veery pooosh.

He looks in her bag. Finds the tissues holds them up. But he's still looking in the bag for some reason.

ANNA. Pass 'em here then.

He lifts a book out of her bag. Inspects it.

Ben!

BEN. Mm?

He throws the tissues towards her. They land on the floor. She stoops to pick them up.

ANNA. Err, thanks!

She clocks what he's doing. Stands up, moves towards him.

What are you doing?

In a not particularly aggressive way, she tries to take the book from his hand. Stronger, he brushes her off.

BEN. What's this?

ANNA. What do you mean what is it? It's a book.

BEN. The *Ladybird Book of Dating*.

ANNA. Yeah it's a joke. They did a series of new Ladybird Books about modern –

BEN. Yeah, I know what it is. I know about the Ladybird Books. I'm ju– (*Struggling a bit to remain good-humoured.*) why have you got it?

ANNA (*taken aback at the interrogation*). Someone bought me it.

BEN. Someone bought you it?

ANNA. Yeah. Erm… Secret Santa.

BEN. Who got you it?

ANNA. It's Secret Santa, Ben! That's the point I don't know. Just someone in the office. Why are you getting worked up about it?

He lets her take the book from his hand.

BEN. I'm just wondering… like why would someone get you that book?

ANNA. It's Secret Santa: you don't choose what you get. It's just random.

BEN. No, it's not random. The point is you choose something befitting of the person you get.

ANNA. Nah, nobody puts any thought in… you just grab something. They have these on the counter at Waterstones. Someone probably just grabbed it and –

BEN. You wouldn't grab that. You might grab the *Ladybird Book of Hipsters* or the *Ladybird Book of Mindfulness,* but '*Dating*'… They must have… you must have…

ANNA. Must have what?

BEN....you must have told them that you're dating.

Pause.

(*Penny dropping.*) You're dating.

BEN *seems faintly shell-shocked. But also calm as if all the misery at least makes sense now somehow.*

ANNA. Well, aren't you?

BEN. No. I mean I tried when we, when we had the break-up. But not like in a fun romcom way. Just in a kinda futile way cos that's what you're supposed to do.

ANNA. I, yeah, me too. It's stressful. And that's why I talk to the girls about it. You must talk to your friends about it.

BEN. Yes, but only to say like 'I went on this date but I just wanted to talk about Anna.' Or 'I've been seeing this girl but she just isn't as good as Anna' or 'I think I only like her because she looks like Anna' or 'She doesn't listen as well as Anna.'

Pause.

ANNA. What about Gillian?

BEN. What about her? She's back with her boyfriend.

ANNA. Oh.

BEN. So no, I'm not dating. I tried it and I failed. So my friends wouldn't have bought me that. They'd have bought me *The Ladybird Book of Not Letting Go of The One*.

Pause.

ANNA. The One?

BEN. Yeah. The One.

Pause.

So who are you dating?

ANNA. Does it matter?

BEN. Just put me out of my fucking misery. Not Seb? Oh don't say you're fucking dating Seb?!

ANNA. No, not Seb. (*Conceding*.) We went on one date. But it was weird. We just ended up talking about the break-up. It's just not a thing.

Pause.

BEN. So who else then?

ANNA. Just guys, random guys: a friend of Tom's, a guy I met at a party, someone off Tinder.

BEN. Right. How… what's your clarity?

ANNA. What's my clarity?

BEN. Yeah, like: what would clarity mean for you? I mean you're dating, so…

ANNA. Erm…

She looks at the bed. Seems much more childlike suddenly.

Maybe I just wanna stay here for ever.

BEN. Maybe you should.

ANNA. But you've gotta home for Christmas. I've gotta go home for Christmas.

BEN. But then we'll come back in the New Year. And then what?

ANNA. So. Oh fucking hell this is hard.

BEN *sits up to listen.*

Something in me feels like it… feels like *of course we should get back together*. I mean I think about you a lot too. I miss not waking up with you. I miss your smell. Sometimes I think I should just leave work in the evening and just turn up here and walk in and not say anything and just take my coat off and get into bed and watch *Breaking Bad*.

BEN. Seen 'em all now. (*Beat*.) But we could watch 'em again. For sure.

ANNA. I think I've come close to doing that. I was going past
the Co-op on the bus one night and I pressed the bell.
I actually pressed the bell. But then I didn't get off.
I stopped myself.

BEN. Why?

ANNA. Well, you might not have been in. Or you might have
been in but… not alone.

BEN *shakes his head dismissively.*

I just think… the reasons we broke up probably haven't gone
away. (*Beat*) Have they?

BEN. Well, I don't remember what they are.

ANNA. You do.

BEN. I don't.

ANNA. I mean you said it. Before the break-up, you said we
had stopped being…

BEN. Curious.

ANNA. Yep. We had stopped being curious about each other.
And I think that's what it comes down to. And now we seem
curious again about each other but I'm worried that soon we
won't be.

BEN. Why?

ANNA. Just… something is telling me we shouldn't go back to
the beginning.

*Pause. She's really battling internally to make sense of
things.*

Like when I think about going back to the beginning there's…
Like an emotional alarm bell. Because we've both still got
a lot ahead of us, adventures and experimenting. And I don't
mean 'sleeping with loads of people', but we're still growing.
As people. Maybe we've taken everything we need from each
other. It's like parting ways, maybe not for ever. But we've
been travelling along side by side for a while and the road has

split and the path is too narrow for – I know that's a lame metaphor. If we stay together the next stage is gonna be just *settling* in a way.

She looks at him for assurance.

BEN. That's what I *want*, Anna.

ANNA (*struggling, soul-searching*). Is it really though? I know you think you're at an age where you should… But thirty's not that old these days… and… *if* we do stay… broken up, then… we'll still be there for each other. You'll meet somebody else. We'll still be friends. You're still my best friend.

BEN. I'm not your fucking friend.

ANNA. What?

He shakes his head.

Ben?

BEN (*really tearing up now though trying not to, emotion impeding his speech*). I'm sorry but I can't be your friend. I'm not your friend. Because if we're not together I couldn't ever see you again. And I don't want to meet anybody else. Because… this is the adventure. (*Pause.*) This is the experiment. This is the brave thing. And yes it's hard. Life is hard. Just being there for another person is hard. At some point you're gonna have to fucking *settle*. You do know that don't you? Not every day of your adult life is gonna be an exciting new treat just popped on to your pillow like a lovely chocolate you know!

ANNA (*slightly patronised*). I know.

BEN (*stern, almost fatherly now*). At some point you're going to have to say 'No, this isn't everything I dreamed about when I was young but it's enough. It's enough for a life. Love is enough.' There's not much love out there you know? It's not an easy fucking thing to come by.

ANNA (*desperate*). But what good is it if it makes you unhappy. You have to admit you were unhappy towards the end.

BEN. But not as unhappy as I am now.

Pause. She says nothing.

I just dunno what to tell you. I feel like there's something
to say like a password or an incantation or just the right
combination of words for me to say to make you see it like
I see it.

ANNA. Ben…

BEN. This is rare, what we have… I can tell you what a rare
woman you are and I'm not just saying this because I'm
fucking selfish and I'm fucking terrified of losing the finest
fucking woman who's ever given me a chance or because
I know that nobody will ever love you like I love you. *This*
is the adventure! I don't need to experiment any more or
sleep with any more people or find myself or find anything
because I've got what I need. You. A life with you. I I can see
it and I need to make you see it. I can – our baby, you in the
hospital bed and our little baby and the beginning of
everything. You with our kids but still being a psychotherapist
and a mum. And me making films. You know, it's a long-term
plan. And in the short term… however we do it, we stay here
tonight and talk about it. Or just we go home for Christmas
and we think more but just tonight isn't the end. Let's just
agree tonight isn't the end.

*He looks at her. She thinks, tries to speak. Almost cries but
doesn't. She shakes her head. He stares desperately,
childishly at her.*

Anna…

ANNA (*almost whispered*). I'm sorry.

He drops his head.

I just…

*He hangs his head, beginning to weep angrily. She tries to
hug him, nuzzle him. He remains unyielding, almost nudges
her away. After a moment she stands up.*

(*Just about holding back tears, voice fragile*.) Better go then.

She moves over to the door, picks up her bag. Notices the jumper on the floor. Picks it up considers it a second.

I was going to erm ask if you wanted this back but maybe I'll… yeah.

She moves towards the door, turns back to him, as if to say something.

Lights down – during the blackout, ANNA *exits into the wings.* BEN *remains standing.*

End.

A Nick Hern Book

Travesty first published in Great Britain in 2016 as a paperback original by
Nick Hern Books Limited, The Glasshouse, 49a Goldhawk Road, London W12 8QP,
in association with Fight in the Dog

Cover illustration by Eleni Kalorkoti

Designed and typeset by Nick Hern Books, London
Printed in the UK by Mimeo Ltd, Huntingdon, Cambridgeshire PE29 6XX

A CIP catalogue record for this book is available from the British Library

ISBN 978 1 84842 615 3

Woodland
CARBON
www.woodlandcarbon.co.uk
NICK HERN BOOKS
Printed on Carbon Captured paper